The Parrot Reckonings
a humorous look at real life with parrots

by

Marguerite Floyd

Address inquires to
Cracked Seed Publishing
PO Box 11365
Lexington KY 40575
info@crackedseedpublishing.com

ISBN 978-0-9856075-3-1

Acknowledgements

Thanks first of all to Phoebe Linden and Liz Wilson for encouraging me, even after they read about the fichus tree incident.

And a special thanks to Carla Thornton (the best editor I've ever worked with) of *Parrot Chronicles*, who not only published my stuff but helped make it actually humorous.

Table of Contents

Introduction

Sugar Franklin, my little lutino cockatiel, changed my life. I know everyone says things like that, but in my case it's true.

I had previously owned zebra finches and assumed a cockatiel would be like a finch, only bigger. It took only a few days before Sugar was educating me. She instigated games with me, fussed when she was displeased, and showed every sign of being smarter than most of the men I've dated.

One evening in our first week together I was at my computer and Sugar Franklin was playing on the desk. I had a bottle of water beside the monitor, with the cap beside it. Sugar began chirping and chirping, and I absently kept telling her she was pretty but I was too busy to pet her. Finally, she picked up the water bottle cap, pranced across my keyboard, and literally threw it on the keyboard. Even I, silly human that I am, knew then that she'd been chirping for water, which I promptly gave her.

While she drank, I realized that I was in way over my head, that this was not some quiet little placid creature like my finches. No, this was a willful bundle of feathers who was quickly going to take over my house if I didn't get myself educated immediately.

It happened that the first book I came across was Mattie Sue Athan's *Guide to a Well-Behaved Parrot*. I learned all manner of things about parrots from that book and even that there were professional people who worked with parrot behavior.

Between the book and Sugar's continuing intelligent behavior I was soon hooked and reading everything I could get my hands on. I sought out listservs about parrots and discovered more people even crazier than me out there.

Since that first week I've become a professional parrot behavior consultant, have written articles for *Bird Talk* and our local bird club, wrote a book about the brown-headed parrot, wrote another book about my life with Sugar Franklin, produced several podcasts about parrot-related things, and set up and operated an online auction site for bird stuff.

I also began writing columns for ParrotChronicles.com – most of which are reprinted in this volume. I actually got fan mail from readers, which was a wonderful new experience for me. So if you like what you read here, feel free to drop me a line (hundred dollar bills are welcome, too!) at mdfloyd@gmail.com

Ten Tough Questions You Should Ask Yourself Before Getting a Parrot

Since my last column, I've been flooded with pertinent questions concerning parrot care and behavior. Here, dear readers, are my impertinent answers.

Q: I'm thinking of getting a parrot. What species is right for me?

A: Excellent question. It depends on what you're looking for in a companion parrot. Do you want one that talks? Can you afford to care for a bird? Do you have mental health insurance? Read on!

Q: Will my bird talk?

A: Your bird most assuredly will be capable of talking. But your bird, individually, will not talk.

Q: I've heard that parrots are messy. Is that true?

A: This is a common myth. In fact, parrots are fastidious by nature. For example, give your bird a piece of paper and it will immediately shred it into dozens of tiny pieces that can be stored in the smallest storage space possible. Parrots are the envy of professional organizers everywhere.

Parrots also keep themselves impeccably groomed. They spend hours each day removing every particle of dust, dander, and loose feather from their bodies. These they distribute over their surroundings in a fine layer of DNA that protects the furniture from scratches.

Q: What size cage should I get?

A: This depends on the species. For example,

macaws require a three-bedroom house. Smaller birds, such as conures, will do fine in a two-bedroom apartment. You and your family will live in the cab of the used pick-up truck you bought after trading in your SUV to pay for foot toys and cinnamon-flavored cooked meals.

Q: What should I feed my new bird?

A: Adequate nutrition is essential for the health of your new family member. Therefore, you should stock your kitchen with grains, vegetables, fruits, and bird pellets. Your bird will not actually eat any of these things, but you must buy them anyway. In time, you will use them to feed your own family, and let me tell you, kids love fruit-flavored Zupreem!

Your bird will eat nacho chips, ice cream, and garlic sticks.

Q: Will my bird bite?

A: Yes. But remember: the more scars you have, especially on the face, the more seriously people will take you as a bird handler. Biting is a self-esteem issue. Yours, not his. Why are you letting a budgie abuse you?

Q: How many toys should I buy my new bird?

A: We are lucky today to have hundreds of sources for safe, entertaining, and educational parrot toys. Experts agree that you should spend a minimum of 90 percent of your disposable income on bird toys.

Once you have filed for bankruptcy, your bird will ignore the new toys and develop a fascination for your universal remote control, which it will groom by removing its buttons.

Q: What kind of medical care will my parrot require?

A: You should take your bird in for a checkup at least every six months. If your bird is exhibiting symptoms of ill health, such as lying on the bottom of his cage with feet in the air, make an appointment with an avian veterinarian immediately. There are a handful of quick and inexpensive diagnostic tests your vet will want to perform. None of these tests will reveal the problem, leaving you to order a dozen of the expensive tests. These tests will prove inconclusive.

Q: How do I bathe my parrot?

A: Parrots love to bathe! Magazines and books are full of pictures of parrots gleefully splashing in the sink. Friends and neighbors will regale you with stories of showering with their birds.

Your parrot will develop a pathological terror of water and will rip your flesh from your bones (see Will My Bird Bite?) if brought near a running faucet. As time goes by, his plumage will take on a bedraggled, unkempt appearance. No matter how well fed he will look like a Chechen orphan. Start looking now for a good lawyer to represent you in court when you're arrested for animal cruelty.

Q: How long will my parrot live?

A: Far longer than you could ever hope for, or desire. Where there's a will, there's a way to stick your brother-in-law with your cranky 85-year-old Amazon after you're gone. That'll teach him to marry into the family! Seriously, talk to your lawyer about setting a little something aside for

Petey's care after your earthly cage-cleaning duties are over. Attach a rider prohibiting the little devil from spending it all on Happy Huts. The way your bird goes through cheese sticks and organic peanuts, he's gonna need it.

We hope this Q&A has been enlightening. Next week we address the oft-asked question, "My husband or my bird?"

How Parrots Wiped Out the Dinosaurs, Befriended Man, and Inspired Harryhausen

Here at ParrotChronicles we often receive e-mails from readers who seek answers to their questions about parrots. We are happy to oblige by drawing on our vast store of knowledge and expertise. My columns have sought to educate on a variety of topics such as how to exercise like a parrot, how parrots compare with computer software applications, understanding the psychological makeup of parrot owners, and how to vote according to your parrot's political affiliation.

Most recently reader Bob White sent us this e-mail: "I was curious about a parrot's role in nature. Some animals are predators; some are seed dispersers. What is the parrot's ecological niche?"

Good question, Bob! The answers are yes, parrots were once predators; yes, parrots are seed dispersers; and yes, parrots fill a niche. How big a niche depends on the size of the bird. Parakeets, for instance, can fall between the sofa cushions if you're not careful. Macaws take up an entire shoulder. Birds spend several hours a day scratching their niches, so yes, parrots play a very important role in our world.

First, some scientific background. According to world-renowned animal expert Dr. Snidewood Tripod, the genus *psittacosis tantrumus rexi* (literally, three impressive Latin-sounding words) encompasses all species of parrot, including those now extinct and those not yet living.

Most scientists believe that *psittacosis*

tantrumus rexi evolved from dinosaurs. However, new findings suggest that parrots were a separate species that was actually responsible for killing off the dinosaurs. In fact, parrots once were predators as large and as fearsome as the T-Rex. The squawks of a 25-foot-tall carnivorous species known as T-Bird could be heard up to 100 miles away.

T-Bird lived during the Psitasic era, when parrots preyed upon shipwrecked sailors and escaped convicts as depicted in *The Seventh Voyage of Sinbad* and *Mysterious Island*, respectively. Some experts have mistakenly identified the birds in Ray Harryhausen films as giant chickens, but what, exactly, is a Roc, after all? Come on, the two-headed bird that flies off with Sinbad in its talons has a hooked beak! Actually, two hooked beaks.

Admittedly, the giant avian of *Mysterious Island*, a freakishly plump bird that winds up as the biggest Thanksgiving dinner ever enjoyed by cast-aways, does resemble a radiated pullet. Still, it's difficult to ignore the ramifications of such large fauna. Where there existed giant chickens there most likely roamed colossal conures as well, and this was only 150 years ago!

As mega fauna became extinct, the parrot emerged in the form of much smaller species that man could tame and keep as pets. In fact, archeological remains have revealed that parrots played a vital role in every civilization known.

The first pet parrots probably wandered into early camps, attracted by the scent of Nutri-berries. In time bird and human came to trust one another and, contrary to the history books, parrots became man's first best friend, riding everywhere on his shoulder and sounding the alarm when saber-toothed tigers approached. Many a Cro-Magnon spent a winter evening gazing into the communal campfire while stroking the head of his faithful cockatiel.

The ancient Egyptians believed parrots were gods; when the birds died they were preserved and entombed in the pyramids along with everything they would need for the afterlife, including Zupreem and Happy Huts.

Before the sacred cow, Hindus revered the sacred cockatoo. The fluffy white birds were allowed to roam the streets, often blocking foot traffic, and perch on whomever they chose. The cockatoo's twice-daily screechings signaled morning and evening prayers.

Parrots have always dominated architecture. Ruins from the pre-neonotredamus period feature colored murals of parrots on each wall of public buildings and in many private residences. In the ancient tropics that came to be known as Antarctica, furnishings and buildings designed for human use were secondary to large multi-branched objects usually located in the center of each area. Carved gutter-like channels leading to outdoor waste water drains were common beneath these large branched objects.

While we could delve further into scientific classifications I think we'd be better off looking at our personal relationships with our parrots. The personal is the political, as the feminists used to say, and I think that applies here.

Today, the parrot is nature's instructor. Just as parrots teach their young what is good to eat and how to identify predators, parrots teach humans how to scritch and provide treats.

Parrots are environmentalists. Long before Al Gore made *An Inconvenient Truth*, parrots were enriching the forest floors and our carpets with half-eaten food to encourage the lush growth of ozone-enhancing foliage. In those instances where no carpet is available, a parrot will chew baseboards in order to admit outside moisture to facilitate growth. Thanks to the parrot's important role in scattering seeds, I personally have witnessed new species of plants sprouting in my shag carpet.

Parrots excel in economics. After learning our primitive system of supply and demand, parrots created an industry for toys, treats, play stands, cages, cage covers, key chains, and more. Consider for a moment an America without the cottage industries of bird toy making or monogrammed hand-sewn cage covers. Yes, it does make you shudder. Even Alan Greenspan refuses to discuss any possibility of a world without parrots' economic contributions.

Finally, we cannot discuss parrots' place in the universe without addressing the spiritual aspect. At one time, as noted above, parrots were worshipped by most cultures, and this worship continues in some of the more remote areas of the world.

Unfortunately, the civilized world has largely forgotten the rich contributions of parrots. Small groups of people, known as "bird clubs," soldier on in an attempt to educate the public. But they only meet monthly, and infighting over the annual bird mart threatens their existence.

If only we could hear the long-ago screeches of the terrible T-Bird as it bore down upon the peaceful brontosaurus, in another time and place. Then perhaps we would know the parrot in its fullness, as predator, as seed disperser, as an influencer of architecture and economics, and, finally, as deity to the innocents, including us.

To summarize, I hope this column has helped you, Bob, and I hope that we continue to hear from ParrotChronicles.com readers.

Remember, there are no stupid questions, only completely irrelevant answers.

How Weird Are Parrot Owners?
Let Us Count the Ways!

What is the matter with you parrot people?

That's how I was thinking of starting this column, but instead I decided on something a bit more subtle. Like, "What peculiar traits do parrot owners share?"

Because, let's face it, parrot people are weird. Now don't deny it or send me indignant notes about how normal you are -- you're not fooling anyone.

Think about it: When a normal person brings a pet such as a dog or a cat or a goldfish into their homes, they continue to lead normal lives. They socialize with other normal people, they continue to listen to the same types of music, read the same types of books, eat the same types of foods as before. You, my parrot-afflicted friend, do not.

So how odd are you? Let's make a list!

You are a scholar of psittacinism.
You scour the Internet and bookstores for research material on parrots. You join discussion groups and share in agonizing detail each tiny movement of your parrot with other parrot owners, who then share a more-than-unusual interest in everyone else's parrot's poop. In fact, poop now occupies so much of your thought and free time that you have lost interest in politics, career, and IRA earnings.

You have begun avoiding normal people, because your parrot seems to have taken a dislike to normal people.
This includes your spouse. When he (or she) walks into the same room as you and your bird, there is obvious resentment at the intrusion. However, you are trying to stop reacting this way.

You eat parrot food.
That is, you have taken to eating the special healthy people food you fix for your parrot. It's so much easier than separately preparing the usual junk for yourself. This is, in general, a good thing. (Just remember to avoid the birdie bread you made with Harrison's.)

You have rearranged your furniture to accommodate your bird and future birds.
If you are severely afflicted, you have bought a new house especially designed for parrotly needs, including vaulted ceilings, screened-in porches, and rooms with drains in the floor.

You buy only healthy and interesting pet toys that cost the equivalent of two months' salary and can be destroyed by a beak in five minutes.
You ask store clerks questions such as, "Is the dye on this wooden block human grade?" and "What types of chemicals were used to treat this suede strip?" and "Where can I find your organic, preservative-free unshelled imported almonds?"

You make your own bird toys.
Sometimes you do this even when you can find bird

toys you like. "My toys are cheaper to make, or more interesting," you tell yourself. Then you set up an Internet store or auction site to sell your toys. You use your other talents For the Good of Parrots. You make quilted cage covers, human clothing protectors, jewelry designed to be worn by humans and chewed on by parrots, paintings of parrots, and key chains engraved with the parrot's name.

Parrots are the dominant species on earth, and they are simply using us to perpetuate their race and eventually take over. If you doubt that, just remember that it's the dominant creature who gets other creatures to take care of it. Think about all you do for your bird, the hours spent cleaning her cage, cleaning the floor, cleaning the food and water dishes, cleaning the bird toys, cooking food, cleaning the walls of said food, bandaging your skin from the latest nip. Then think about how you sit down exhausted and feel grateful and honored to look upon her pampered plumage and big dark eyes.

This is not normal. You'll never see a dog person made misty by the beauty of their pet slowly lifting its leg.

I say it's high time we parrot people reclaim our lives and save the human race from certain demise. Be strong -- it won't be easy or done quickly, but by acting together we can thrive as a species again.

I'll be right there with you, just as soon as I finish sewing this bird cosey and taking the pellet casserole out of the oven.

If Parrots Were Software Programs, Windows Would be Toast

After wasting a perfectly good weekend attempting to network my old Macintosh computer with my new Macintosh computer, I finally surrendered to the will of the Great Computer Spirit and gave up. However, while untangling the 857 cables and wires that had taken over my desk, I began to wonder about parrots. More specifically, if a parrot were a computer software program, what kind would it be?

After a lengthy, in-depth two-minute discussion of this with a friend, we came to the following conclusions:

African greys are Microsoft Project, a scheduler and project planner. Greys are always planning something, thinking and scheming of how best to accomplish their missions.

Amazons are Quicken, a personal finance program. Amazons are always calculating and keeping track.

Budgies are Microsoft Outlook Express, a lightweight e-mail program. Budgies like to talk, are quick on their feet, and don't take up a lot of space.

Cockatiels are Linux, an independent computer operating system. They are eccentric, with no sense of humor, and frequently suffer from lack of publicity.

Cockatoos are the viruses of the parrot world. They love to destroy things for no reason other than that they can and you can't do a thing about it except try to repair the damage.

Conures would be spammers, infiltrating your household. They're always busy and into everything, sneaking up on you at random times and screeching about the latest whatever.

The eclectus is, of course, a virus scanner. It sits and watches, always prepared to take over when necessary.

The kakapo is Windows, but only because it's flightless and weighs a whopping eight pounds. (If I were to put a kakapo on my hard drive, it would take up lots more space than, say, a disk utility like a love bird. See below.) Very much unlike Windows, the kakapo is not everywhere you turn (if only it were Windows and not the kakapo that faces extinction). And wouldn't it be nice if Windows had a fruity smell?

Lorikeets are the clipboard. They're messy and "paste" things wherever they want, without regard to organization.

Love birds are disk utilities, such as a hard disk defragmentation program. They don't take up much space, but they're tenacious and keep things in order.

Macaws are networks. They transmit information over long distances.

Parrotlets are personal firewalls. They are wary, bitey, protective, and aggressive. Nothing gets past them.

Quakers are databases. They like to build huge, complicated nests of interrelated twigs.

Senegals, of course, would be the new Macintosh operating system – thoughtful, enjoying an upside down view of the world, with many new, yet-to-be discovered features.

Once I was able to relate my personal computers to parrots, I felt much better. I finally got those cables untangled and I might even try networking my two Macs again. Then again, I could just spend next weekend playing with my birds.

I'm Too Busy to Have a Normal Life Anymore;
I Have Parrots, You Know

The few non-bird-owning friends I have left often express surprise, even alarm, as to what I might be doing in my spare time. I was once known as a woman who was always prompt, who accomplished whatever tasks needed doing, the one who always organized the next yard sale or gathered signatures for a petition. Someone you could depend on.

Now? Well, let's just say that now I bear more than a passing resemblance to one of those fascinating individuals whose lives have shrunk to orbit a much smaller universe, a world they have created to support the one all-consuming passion that has taken over their existence. For some it's Irish dancing, for others it's knitting or Civil War battle reenactments.

For me, it's parrots. While all my non-bird-owning friends spend their spare time wind-surfing, volunteering at the hospital, and planning trips to the Caribbean (after helming $50 million corporations, writing movie scripts, and raising 2.5 children), you will find me catering to the needs of three cockatiels and a brown-head parrot. It goes something like this:

5 - 6:45 a.m. Up and at 'em to prepare organic grains. Good nutrition is vital for shiny feathers! While breakfast is simmering on the stove I awaken my darlings with the gentle reverie of slipping the hand-made covers off their cages. I believe in spending as much quality time with my

birds as possible before I leave for work.

Sugar Franklin, the lutino cockatiel, rewards me with a stretch of her gorgeous yellow wings. Or, depending on her mood, a hair-raising hiss that means "how dare you disturb my slumber, lowly woman servant. Replace the sleeping cover at once!"

I can depend on Flash to hiss and lunge at me through the bars of his cage. Ever since I added another male cockatiel (Nicholas) to the household, Flash has been angry, understandably so. I gently whistle a short tune to him to show I still love him. He lunges again. If he were a saber tooth tiger, a fang would now be impaling my neck. Flash's nemesis, Nicholas, bless his heart, sticks his little head against the cage bars for a scratch. Isn't that sweet? I accept the invitation and get snapped at in return.

Charli pops her head out of her sleeping hut and looks so warm and fluffy and cuddly it's all I can do not to grab her and kiss her all over. Sometimes she'll offer a good morning chirp and then go back to sleep like any sensible creature. This is the most social time of the day for her.

The organic grains have finished cooking. I dish up the cereal into separate bowls for each bird. I blow on each bowl for a couple of minutes to make sure the food is not too hot.

While the birds toss their breakfast on the floor, I run through the shower and throw on the first thing I find in my closet. Before dashing out the door I turn on the television so the birds won't miss Dr. Phil.

7 – 4 p.m. Work to pay for mortgage, food,

and bird accessories.

4:45 p.m. Carrying mail, purse, paperwork brought home from the office, and groceries, I stagger through the front door and call out a greeting to my beloved parrots.

With nine hours to consider her earlier behavior, Sugar has seen the error of her ways and is genuinely glad to see me. She screams and runs back and forth on her perch as if turbocharged by one of the better classes of amphetamines while I dump everything on the dining room table, whose surface no one has seen since the first Clinton inauguration. I open Sugar's cage and she happily climbs out onto my finger. I give her a peck on her beak and she pecks me back on the nose.

With Sugar on my shoulder I open Charli's cage and invite her to come out. "Come on, Charli! Come out, sweetie! Come see Mommy!" Sometimes she is not impressed with my arrival and sits on her high perch as if made of stone. "Come out, baby! Come out, Charli!" No, Charli has seen Medusa and tragically, has been turned into a pillar of salt.

On her non-sodium days, Charli will slowly and delicately move toward the cage door. When I open it, she backs or turns away from me as if noticing for the first time I have insufferably bad breath. "Up, Charli," I say. "Come see Mommy!"

Charli will consider this request, perhaps taking a reluctant step or two toward me, and then, remembering my bad dental hygiene, she moves off to the far corner of the cage. "Come on, Charli." I tap my finger against the cage door. I wait a moment, then in my sternest voice, "I'm going to leave you in there." Charli considers this for a long while, so long that I usually give up. I make a big show of closing the cage door and turning my attention to the cockatiels.

I open their doors and Nicholas immediately climbs into Flash's cage. A great deal of hissing commences, then the two rivals settle into mutual preening, punctuated by the occasional accidentally tweaked feather and hissing from the offended party.

I return to plea with Charli. Finally she saunters out, being sure to sink her sharpened nails into my flesh. This reminds me: it's grooming day at the vet's! I can't be late this time. I hate the look the receptionist gives me even more than the creepy stares every feline patient in the room trains on my birds the minute we walk in.

I quickly change from my work clothes into something more casual for the vet's. Which fashion statement should I make today? The t-shirt with a dozen small holes for the moth-eaten look favored by most bird owners? Or the stained t-shirt for that Jackson Pollack splashed-poo look? I decide ragged is less offensive.

I find the four small travel cages and spend 30 minutes convincing, threatening, and finally forcing each bird into its respective carrier. Then it's out to the car, arranging all the cages in the front and back seats, and strapping them in. I get halfway down the street before I realize I've forgotten my purse. Late again.

6:30 p.m. Grooming over, it's back home for dinner and baths! Sugar prefers to be misted in the kitchen sink, but only after examining every inch of the surrounding counters to be sure they do not contain any stray Nutriberries. Charli does not like baths of any sort, so I must spend 20 minutes chasing her around the kitchen before she gives up and tolerates a few sprinkles of water. Flash is unsure about any water that does not appear in a ceramic bowl and shivers miserably under the mist. Nicholas, my water baby, prefers to be held under a running faucet.

7:15 p.m. While the birds are back in their cages, preening their wet feathers, I prepare their dinner, which consists of fresh or defrosted frozen vegetables (hey, it can't be filet mignon every night). I serve them in separate bowls, then stand back to watch as my birds throw their vegetables on the floor and stare at me for more. Which I promptly provide. I microwave a frozen dinner for myself.

8 p.m. Time to give each bird their own special time with me! Sugar demands scritches alternating with sinking her beak into my fingers because I'm not doing it to suit her. When my fingers are numb from bites, I return her to her cage. If she isn't too angry with me for scritching Sugar first, Charli will come out of her cage and allow me to pet her. We then play an amusing game of Charli climbing onto my shoulder and me removing her from my shoulder. While on my shoulder she uses the opportunity to clean her beak on my t-shirt. If the phone happens to ring, I have to let the machine pick up. The telephone receiver is a dangerous beast, and Charli will lay her life on the line to protect me from it, even if it means piercing my ear to prevent the monster from approaching my face.

If all the birds are in their cages, they chirp happily while I talk, usually at top volume. With the sound of Flash and Nicholas hissing added to the cacophony, people on the other end often ask what that "noise" is.

For some reason I bring Flash and Nicholas out together for their quality time, placing them on separate shoulders. When I attempt to pet one, the other hisses, causing the pet-ee to fly off my shoulder and career through the house, ending up on top of the window blinds or under a table. This startles the other bird, who flies into a different part of the house. There commences much shrieking between the two cockatiels as they attempt to locate each other while making sure to stay just out of my reach.

By the time each bird has had their "special time" with me, the evening news, the weather, and latest episode of my favorite sitcom are history. I tell myself that if anything important has happened in the world someone will mention it at work tomorrow.

8:45 p.m. It's time to wipe down the cages, change the papers, replenish the water bottles, and give each bird fresh pellets. Each bird receives its own special nighttime treat, of course, such as millet or Nutriberries. Sometimes I even remember to prepare dishes of frozen veggies to thaw out in the refrigerator for the next morning. I cover all the cages, stopping to say special sweet things to each of them. All the cockatiels bid me goodnight with a hearty hiss. Charli says nothing.

9:15 p.m. I go into the study to check my e-mail. My chair tilts dangerously because Charli has been gnawing at its legs and removing the bolts. Someone on a bird list mentions a new toy their parrot just loves. I Google it until I find it for sale in a small shop in Madagascar. I order four, change my mind and order eight -- just in case it's a big hit with all the birds.

10 p.m. Exhausted, I collapse on the couch, kick off my shoes, and suddenly remember I was supposed to meet someone at 7 to discuss an important project. I call to apologize, knowing full well how ridiculous I sound, stammering on about losing track of the time because of my parrots.

After all, how involved could it be to take care of a few birds?

The Full-Service Pet Sitter: Cage Washer, Gourmet Chef, and All-Around Perfect Nanny

It was a simple matter. I'd paid my money to share a cabin with some friends at a state park right on the ocean, and I'd be leaving town on a Monday in late April.

All I needed was to set the dates with my usual bird sitter, Alice. (Note: All names have been changed at the insistence of the guilty.)

Alice is a vet tech at my avian vet's office and while she charges an arm and a leg, she's very good and I trust her with my babies. She comes over twice a day to change the papers, feed goodies, take the birds out for play time, and just generally spoil them. I suspect she also gives them ideas of things they can do to torment me when I return, but I haven't been able to prove that yet.

Plus, Alice is an excellent vet tech. She not only knows what constitutes an emergency, she also knows what to do in one, unafraid to administer syringes of medication if necessary. I'm very fond of Alice, but don't tell her that or she'll raise her rates.

The first week of March I called Alice and told her when I needed her to bird sit. For a long moment I heard pages flipping. Finally she said, "According to my calendar, I'll be out of town then."

"What?"

"I'm going to a seminar. It's out of town."

"But I need you to bird sit for me." It was incomprehensible to me that Alice has a life outside the vet's office or my home. She's told me before that she has her own home, but I don't believe she lives anywhere but the vet's office.

"Well, I'm sorry, but I have to be out of town."

She didn't sound very sorry to me, so I persisted. "But I've already paid for everything and I can't cancel. Who's bird sitting for *you*?" Alice has several birds of her own, though they're not nearly as pretty and charming as my birds.

"Kathy is housesitting for me. I could ask her if she'd want to check on your birds."

What choice did I have? I sighed. "OK, would you please ask her and get back to me? Or shall I ask her?"

"Better let me ask her, " Alice said.

Of course, I could have taken my birds to one of the local pet stores or to another vet for boarding, but they don't get any attention and it's a strange place to them. My regular vet no longer boards birds, so that leaves me at the mercy of people like Alice.

A couple of days later, Alice called to inform me that Kathy would have her hands full and wouldn't be able to bird sit for me.

I was ready to beg at this point. "Well, what am I going to do?" It was clearer to me than ever that this was all Alice's fault.

Alice thought for a moment. "You might call Jane Smith. She bird sits sometimes."

"You understand," I told Alice, "that you are never, ever to leave town again without checking with me first, don't you?"

Alice laughed. She obviously didn't know I was serious.

Jane Smith is one of only five federally licensed wildlife rehabilitators in our state, specializing in birds, and she's also a member of the local bird club. I called another member of the bird club to check out her work. When I received glowing reports about her, I called Jane.

The first thing Jane asked was, "How often do you want the cages cleaned?"

Clean the cages? It never occurred to me to ask a bird sitter to clean my bird cages. "Well, I change the papers every other day or more often if they've been eating something messy."

"I asked because some people want me to dismantle and completely clean the cages everyday. You've got four birds and I just don't have time to do all that. I'm coming into my busy season, you know."

I immediately assured her I just wanted someone to check on the birds, be sure they had fresh water and food, maybe play with them a little, and not let them run up my phone bill. Jane gave this some thought, then asked what sort of vegetable regimen I had them on.

Vegetable regimen? "Well," I said, "they get whatever vegetables I eat in my TV dinners during the week, plus whatever I happen to cook on the weekends. Plus pasta and Nutriberries and the occasional blueberry or broccoli stalk. They're all on Harrison's, of course."

I could hear Jane frown. "Birds need lots of veggies and I love to see them eat. I fix about a hundred servings of veggies and corn bread and nuts for all my birds every day." I could hear her hundred or so birds in the background, so I didn't doubt it. Of course, it was also obvious that Jane didn't have a job or much else outside her home.

"If you can get my birds to eat veggies, by all means you have my permission to do so."

We made arrangements for Jane to come meet my birds and confirm all the details. I liked Jane immediately, though I doubted her ridiculous "vegetable regimen" idea would have any effect whatsoever on my birds. I foresaw numerous carpet stains from tossed vegetables and mushy blueberries. I silently vowed to make Alice pay for her treachery.

When I finally arrived at the cabin to start my vacation, I immediately called Jane to be sure she'd gotten into my house all right. She was enthusiastic and assured me that she'd gotten in just fine. "I brought them cornbread and lots of cut-up vegetables. Sugar Franklin loves corn and cornbread. They all dived right in and ate up everything."

"That's great," I said, but I had to wonder if she was in the right house. My birds have never dived right into a bowl of anything but Cheerios. I left Jane my number in case of an emergency and said I wouldn't call again unless something came up. That was on Monday afternoon.

By Wednesday I missed my birds so much I broke down and called Jane. "They're all fine," she said. She went on to tell me how Sugar Franklin adores cornbread and corn and carrots and lettuce, how Charli couldn't wait for her grapes and green beans, how even the other two cockatiels eagerly chowed down on their mixed vegetables.

"It's easy," Jane said. "You just put

everything out in fridge in the evenings to thaw, and all you have to do in the mornings is put the bowls in their cages before you leave for work. I usually make a big batch of cornbread on Sundays."

While I was glad my birds were fine and eating like kings, I also began to worry. Jane was spoiling them rotten. Would I have a riot on my hands when I returned? Would the birds go on a hunger strike if I didn't prepare cornbread everyday? Would they stalk me for green beans almondine, scream bloody murder for carrots julienne every morning? If I didn't deliver, would Jane report me to the Humane Society? Would I get kicked out of the bird club?

While I didn't get much rest on my vacation for worrying, I am pleased to report that my birds still love me and even acted glad when I got home. Jane's veggie regimen, alas, is no more. I don't know why. Just like she told me to, I leave thawed-out mixed veggies in the mornings before I go to work. But when I get home in the evening, I find most of the veggies untouched.

Maybe Jane ate veggies with the birds, and they chowed down just to be polite. Maybe she handfed tidbits to them over the course of hours, cooing and praising with each successful bite. Perhaps I should quit my job so I can spend all day offering them veggies by hand.

But the important thing is that now I have two bird sitters from which to choose, should I ever be able to afford to be away from home overnight again. And Jane, bless her heart, has set a new standard for bird sitting.

Now that I know daily cage cleaning and diet

consultations are options, I wonder what else is available. Does anyone out there offer French lessons? (I've always dreamed of Charli learning one of the Romance languages!) How about macramé, ceramics, aikido? Perhaps Charli could learn a more useful form of woodworking than reducing my living room furniture to splinters. For that matter, surely someone can teach them how to make their own cornbread to save me the trouble.

I'm so glad I found Jane. She has opened me and my birds to a whole new world of possibilities. I expect that within a couple of years, Sugar Franklin, Charli, and the cockatiels will be fully qualified to enter the best Ivy League colleges. Then I'll have them out of my hair long enough to take lots of vacations on the beach. Thanks, Jane!

Out of My Tree: My Birds Frolicking in a Fichus? Yeah, Right!

So Phoebe Linden, the bird behavior expert, was telling us to get a fichus tree for our birds to play in. Only $20 at Home Depot, as some kind lady who sat next to me at the luncheon said. Nothing to it!

The Monday after returning home from Phoebe's seminar in Pittsburgh, I headed over to Home Depot. I did not know exactly what a fichus tree looked like. I wandered over to the "foliage assortment" display and finally came upon something called a Snow Fichus.

Two tiny little trees, plants really, with white-centered leaves. Way too small for the two birds I had at the time: Charlie, my brown-headed parrot, and maybe even Sugar Franklin, a cockatiel. But it was a start. I touched one of the trees and approximately 40 leaves fell off.

I glanced around to see if any of the staff had witnessed this phenomenon, but I was safe. So safe, in fact, that I had to walk over to plumbing to find someone to help me.

Eventually, some guy about 14 years old led me back to the "foliage assortment" display and pulled out a fichus (or, as the tag said, fig tree). It was perhaps four feet tall and had maybe 20 leaves on it.

"This is all we have left," he told me, "but there's another shipment due any day now."

"Ah," I said, considering the dry potted earth as yet another leaf drifted to the floor. "Are they all about this size?"

"You can get bigger," he assured me, not realizing I was more interested in bushiness than height. "Call us later today to see if the new ones have come in yet."

I said I would, made a mental note never to call them again, and headed over to Lowe's.

Lowe's, unlike Home Depot, is famous for never having anyone available to help you do or find anything, including checking out. But they do have a slightly larger greenhouse. I saw a pleasant-looking woman near the light bulbs and trapped her. "I need a fichus tree," I said, looking as pitiful as possible.

"Well, sure," she said, very politely. That should have been a warning. She led me to the greenhouse and a huge display of trees that she assured me were ficuses.

"It's for my parrots," I told her, as if every customer that came in had parrots and fichus trees were created for them. She smiled and took a tentative step backward.

"So which of these are good fichus trees? And how would I know?" She hmmmm'd for a moment and said, "You know, actually I'm just a vendor. Let me get you a clerk." At that point I noticed that she did have a label on her coat that said, "Vendor." My heart sank because I knew she would disappear, and I would be left standing there until closing time.

But the home-improvement store gods were smiling on me and a real live Lowe's clerk appeared. She was the garden specialist and told me that whichever fichus tree I got would immedi-ately be traumatized and lose much of its leaves and that when I repotted, it would lose even more. She showed me the $45 fichus trees and asked if I was interested in braided ornate trunks.

"Uh, just something simple for my parrots," I said. She frowned and said perhaps the "sale" fichus might be more suitable, though she doubted they could hold a parrot.

"They're small parrots," I told her. "Just something for them to play in."

She ignored this additional bit of information and watched while I pulled out a specimen about 4 1/2 feet tall that seemed to have most of its leaves.

It also seemed to be L-shaped. I asked the clerk about this and she assured me that it was the pot that was crooked. To prove this, she wiggled the pot back and forth. It was only $6.96, so I felt pleased at getting such a bargain. I also got a bigger pot to repot it so that it could be doubly traumatized all at once. Altogether, my purchase was less than $12.

I lugged the tree and pot out to my Geo Prism and opened the back door. To get the tree to fit inside, I had to remove junk from the back floorboard, put the tree on the floor, and gently bend the top half. Several leaves fell off during this process.

I went immediately home, reversing the process of bending the tree to get it out of the car, causing several more leaves to fall off.

After getting the tree inside, I realized I had no room in my house for a tree. Even my parrots knew this -- they watched in horror from the safety of their cages as I carefully put down newspaper and placed the tree here and there, over on that side and this, perhaps if I moved the lamp . . . .

Several leaves fell off during this process. I had part of a big bag of dirt left over from my last failed attempt at gardening, so I put some of that into the new pot, stuck the tree in, and put the rest of the dirt on top of it.

I stood back to admire my work and saw that the tree was still L-shaped and bent at a 45 degree angle -- even though it was now in the new, non-wobbly pot. I rearranged the dirt to shore up the "weak" side, but the tree still leaned, as if determined to provide its own awning.

Several leaves fell off during this process. I ended up putting the tree, at its jaunty slant, between the finch's cage and the television. I added some water to the pot, which immediately ran out over the brim of the collection pan, onto the five layers of newspaper, and into my carpet. I spent the next 20 minutes blotting up water, changing newspapers, and considering a better place to put the tree.

Perhaps in the study, I thought. I lugged the now 50-pound tree into the study and then realized that the room was too dim during the day when I'm at work. So back into the living room, beside the TV. My neck had been bothering me for several days and lifting and moving the tree was sending my nerve endings into number 14 on the 1-to-10 pain scale.

I sat down to assess the damage and swallow a handful of ibuprofen. This was the point at which both Charli and Sugar Franklin let me know in no uncertain terms that they did not like this tall, oddly slanted thing in the living room. They peered at it from the farthest reaches of their cages, squawked several times, and kept looking at me. Would I move it again?

I took them out of their cages, put them on my shoulder, and stood a respectful distance from the tree. "This is your tree," I told them. "Pretty soon you'll be playing in its branches and having a wonderful time." They shrank back further on my shoulder.

Over the next few weeks, the birds watched me carefully vacuum up clods of dirt around the fichus and saw that it did not move or attack me. Sugar Franklin took a tentative nibble on one of the leaves and discovered that she liked it.

The fichus tree, of course, dropped several of its leaves in response.

The other day Carl, the kindly retired man who's taken pity on my pitiful yard and does gardening for me at greatly reduced rates, stopped by to pick up a check.

I pointed out the fichus tree in the living room, still leaning over from the weight and trials of having dropped almost all of its leaves, and asked him if it was dead yet. He fingered the bare branches and snapped one off.

Carl said that fichus trees were awfully hard to keep. I showed him how the soil was still damp, despite the pot draining properly and me not having watered it in several weeks. He shook his head sadly. Best to let it go, he said.

After he left, I gave the tree a good shake and took it out to back deck to brave the cold weather. I didn't have the heart to just throw it out. Not yet.

So there it sits outside my kitchen window, mocking me with its one or two bright green leaves flapping in the wind. The wild birds that visit my bird feeder avoid it, too, just as my indoor birds did.

Paris Thinks It's Tough Milking Cows?
Let Her Try Being a Bird Owner for One Day!

I'm not all that impressed with reality shows. Oh sure, those people out in the jungle might smell after a few days or may eat a few worms, but that's a small price to pay for a chance at a million bucks.

Take the latest reality show, "The Simple Life." Hotel heiress Paris Hilton and best friend Nicole Richie (daughter of legendary pop star Lionel Richie) are forced to spend a month on an Arkansas farm, milking cows and going to quilting bees. Like this is hard? Give me a break!

I have an idea for my own reality show. I call it "The Seedful Life." In my show, Paris Hilton comes to my house and takes care of my parrots for a day. Just one day.

Join in on the hilarity as Paris (her pal Nicole ain't up for this one) leaves behind the comforts of her lavish lifestyle in Los Angeles for a chance to live the life of a bird owner. Armed with her Louis Vuitton bag and her teacup Chihuahua, Tinkerbelle, she struggles to make the transition from the penthouse to the birdhouse. Four birds. One suburban home. One sink for washing food bowls. One haughty self-indulgent airhead model-slash-actress. Together they add up to one side-splitting day!

Let's look in on Paris and see how she's faring with Charli the African brown-headed parrot and the cockatiels Sugar, Nicholas, and Flash.

6:45 a.m. Paris and Tinkerbelle arrive and I explain the job. I want Paris to uncover the bird cages, feed the birds, change their papers, play with them, and feed them again by the time I get home at four. Paris stares blankly, pops her gum. Her brow furrows. "You mean, like, I have to touch them?" I cross myself and leave for work.

7 a.m. Paris whips the covers off the cages and greets the birds with a bright "Hello!" Their sleep interrupted, the birds stare back sullenly, except for Nicholas, who wolf whistles.

7:05 a.m. Exhausted from her efforts, Paris wobbles into the living room on her three-inch platforms and flops down on the sofa. She grabs the remote control and tunes in "Am I Hot?" The cockatiels begin their "breep, breep!" call for breakfast. "Will you SHUT UP?" Paris shouts from the living room, annoyed. After turning the volume all the way up, she gives up and decides to get the chores over with.

7:10 a.m. Paris stands in front of the cages, manicured hands on hips. "Okay, birds. I'm supposed to do this newspaper thing." She peers inside one of the cockatiel cages and wrinkles her nose. "Ewwww!" She picks up Tinkerbelle, who has not stopped trembling since their arrival. "Thank goodness I have my Tinky Winky with me! You're not disgusting, are you, Tinky? You're not like these nasty old parakeets." She finds rubber gloves in the kitchen and, pinching her nostrils shut with one hand, changes the papers with the other. This takes the better part of an hour because Paris must pause every few seconds to gag.

8 a.m. After taking a long hot shower to wash off the bird cooties, Paris feels better. Good enough, in fact, to tackle feeding the birds. When

she opens the last cage door to pour pellets into the food bowl, a cockatiel escapes. As Nicholas flies tight circles around the room, Paris shrieks and ducks. "Stay away! Stay away from me! Tinky, run! Run, Tinky, run!"

9 a.m. Her migraine much better, Paris tiptoes back to the door of the bird room and opens it a crack. Nicholas is back in his cage. Paris rushes into the room and slams his cage door shut.

10 a.m. Lying on the couch, Paris flips open her cell phone. "You gotta see this," she tells Nicole, and snaps a picture of my living room. "Bird seed everywhere. It's totally revolting. How can anyone live like this?" Paris stares up at the ceiling. "This is sooooo boring. Are you sure you can't come over? Nicole? Nicole??"

Noon. Paris goes to the Dairy Queen for lunch. "Tell your sons I'm single and in town for another four hours," she announces before winking at the cashier and sashaying out. "Who was that?" the manager asks. "Marguerite Floyd's bird sitter," the cashier replies. "You know, from that new reality show, 'The Seedful Life.'"

2 p.m. Bored out of her skull, Paris decides to do something fun. She will let all the birds out of their cages so they can play together. She opens all the cage doors and steps back to the center of the room. "Okay, birds, free time. Just don't fly over my head. That creeps me out." Charli, whose mission in life is to eradicate cockatiels, happily scoots out of her cage and onto Flash's, so she can ambush him when he comes out. Sugar and Nicholas make a beeline for Paris' blonde head. "Get off me! Get off!" Paris screams, swatting at them. She totters into the

living room, where Sugar alights on her arm and with one deft motion chomps through an expensive bracelet, sending beads and bangles tinkling to the floor. Nicholas scores a runny one through Paris' open-toed sandals.

Paris limps whimpering to the bathroom to clean up. When she bends down with a Kleenex, the cockatiels land on her back, hiss at one another, and begin to beak fight. Paris twists every which way trying to dislodge them. Flash lands on her shoulder and screams.

3 p.m. Still partially deaf in one ear, Paris tries to gather up the cockatiels with a broom and dustpan, but they skitter under the dining room table. Paris tries to pick up Charli but Charli bites her. Paris drops Charli, falls off a platform, and twists her ankle. "I can't believe this is happening to me!" she wails. "Tinky! Tinky! Come on, we're getting out of here!" Tinkerbelle is nowhere to be found. "Tinky? Tinkerbelle? Where are you?" Checking the back yard, Paris finds Tinkerbelle *in flagrante delicto* with the dachshund from next door. An anguished scream echos through the streets.

4 p.m. I arrive home as Paris is being wheeled away on a gurney with an IV in her arm. She's dazed, bleeding, hair sticking up in tufts, makeup streaked, ankle elevated. "Did you have a good time, honey?" I ask, suspecting I already know the answer. "What kind of hellhole do you live in, lady?" Paris growls. "I'm suing you, your parakeets, and Fox. Some things are just too hideous for one person to endure." As they load her in the ambulance Paris flips open her cell phone one last time

and sobs into it. "Oh, Nicole, it was awful. It was just like that movie. Yeah, that's the one. 'The Birds.' Make us dinner reservations at the Hilton. I'm coming home."

Parrot Lover's Exercise Regimen:
Staying in Shape is for the Birds!

I'm at that age (and weight) where doctors like to talk to me about the importance of exercise and a healthy diet and while they're at it stick various implements into my body where implements do not naturally go.

They're right, of course, and in deference to them I've designed the perfect exercise regime for all parrot lovers based on the activities of my parrots. You should speak to your own parrots and probably a human doctor or at least a decent vet before beginning any exercise program.

We begin with the all-important stretch. Standing on both feet, slowly lift one arm and the corresponding leg and foot behind you at the same time. Lean an inch or so forward as you do this. Hold for about 30 seconds. Repeat with the other arm and foot (after putting the first foot back on the ground, of course). Not only will this stretch and warm up your muscles, it will also air out your armpits, for which your housemates will be grateful.

Too many exercise programs neglect the facial muscles, but my parrots have the perfect solution. Periodically, scratch your ear with your toes and then yawn eight times in rapid succession. Sneezing may occur during this exercise and should be encouraged. If you're not feeling very cheerful lean your head forward a little, slick down the hair (or skin) on your head, and hiss at the nearest object/person; this will strengthen those all-important air passages.

While we're in the neighborhood of the face, let's not forget the eyes. Turn your head 90 degrees to either side and stare at something, preferably something no one else can see. Do not blink or move. Keep staring for up to three minutes without moving.

To give those neck muscles a real workout, turn your head 180 degrees and preen the skin (or hair, as the case may be) on your back. When you've finished with your back, turn your head back around and preen the skin (or hair) on your chest, working downward to your toes. To finish up, run those long strips of skin (or hair) of your tail through your beak . . . er, teeth. This exercise not only helps your neck but will add luster to your teeth. As an added bonus, try to perform this exercise while sitting on someone's shoulder to enhance your balancing skills.

Speaking of teeth, lip grinding is a nice way to relax. Simply rub your lips (and teeth, if you desire) against each other until you're making a weird noise. It often helps to halfway close your eyes during this.

For those times you're bored, nothing beats a session of heavy arm flapping. It's more enjoyable if there is a lot of loose paper and dust around when you do this, too.

After strenuous exercise you'll want to have a nice bath. Fill the tub with an inch of tepid water and step in. Dip your head into the water and fling it over your back. It helps if you have long hair, but even bald people can do this. Bend your elbows and use a flapping motion to distribute the water all over your body. To dry off, commence preening or wait for someone to wrap you in a towel.

Before leaving the tub, don't forget to take a few long sips of bathwater. It's important that you get enough liquids through the day, and there's no sense in dirtying up a glass when there's perfectly wet water right in front of you, now is there?

My favorite, though, is the five o'clock screech. When I get home from work my parrots greet me with loud bouts of screaming. After the kind of day I usually have at work I always join right in. Sometimes even the neighbors like to stop by during these sessions. I promise this exercise will make everyone feel better.

So there you have it -- the perfect all-body exercise regime for those of us who live with parrots. Repeat all of these exercises daily, and before you know it your doctor will be talking to you about special care reserved for very special people!

Cleaning Up is for the Birds

Not long ago I was home from work with a nasty case of bronchitis. As the drugs began working and I began to slowly mend, I noticed the carpet. It was awful -- seeds, tiny bits of tissue, teeny tiny bits of wicker from Shredders and toys, slivers of wood from chewable toys. I knew it would make me feel better to spend three minutes to vacuum it up. So I did. And promptly ran the vacuum over a piece of the cockatiels' play basket. At which point the vacuum cleaner belt broke.

But it was okay because I was sure I didn't have any belts, and I certainly wasn't going out to get one. However, when I opened the closet door to put the vacuum away, there was a bag of two brand new belts. I cursed myself for being prepared and having spare parts in case I need them. I vaguely recalled changing belts on this cleaner before and in my memory it didn't seem so traumatic. So I trudged the cleaner back out along with the belts.

The birds watched this with great interest, cocking their heads to be sure to take in the entire process.

I considered sitting on the floor to work on the vacuum, but then I remembered how old I am. I sat down at the dining room table. Of course, I had to get up again to get the wrong screwdriver.

I looked over the directions in the manual again. It shouldn't be too difficult. (Yes, I keep appliance manuals forever. I am most attached to those manuals that go with appliances that no longer exist in my house or anywhere else in the universe. Any day now one of them will sell on eBay for millions, and I'll be ready.)

Sitting again at the table I flipped the cleaner over. There were no screws where the manual insisted they were. There were, however, two screws in places the manual didn't include in the helpful diagram. I unscrewed those. The body of the cleaner wouldn't budge. I tugged and pulled and cursed until I heard a sickening screech of plastic against plastic as the cover came off.

I found feathers sticking out of the motor. I found long threads from those piñata toys wrapped tightly around the rollers. I found half of a Nutri-berri in the casing. I found thick coatings of seeds and millet husks firmly attached to everything with grease.

The roller would not budge, so I used the wrong screwdriver and persistence until the roller finally popped out of its brackets. The broken belt easily slipped off, coating my greasy hands with lint and more feathers.

I put the new belt on, but it seemed to be six inches too short. Somewhere behind me I thought I heard a whisper of an avian snicker. I spun around to see who was laughing at me, but the birds were innocently preening. I double-checked the bag to be sure I'd actually bought the correct size.

I slipped one end of the roller into its bracket. I then put my foot on the roller and pulled and pulled on the belt until I was able to stretch it around the roller, which was not easy since my hands were coated with black grease and the belt kept slipping. Whereupon the other end of the roller popped out. I sat back to catch my breath and consider the situation.

I'm happy to say that after only five tries I did manage to get both ends of the roller into the brackets, only to realize I'd forgotten to secure the belt around the roller. The snickering seemed to grow louder.

Once the matter of the roller and belt was taken care of, it was just a simple matter of replacing the cover. Unfortunately the cover seemed to have grown larger while it sat on the floor, sprouting extra angles. But I was stronger than the cover and wrestled it into place, more or less. I lost a screw but no matter -- I had the belt replaced. And how important could one little screw be anyway?

The snickering sounded louder this time. I spun around to catch them in the act, but the birds were nonchalantly eating.

Now that the belt was in I took it for a test run. Nothing. The cleaner was too high off the floor. I fiddled with some levers and got the thing closer to the floor and mostly got the carpet clean -- or at least presentable. But that wasn't good enough. I stomped on the cleaner to move it closer to the floor, though better of it, and then climbed onto the cleaner so that my entire weight would move the cleaner to the correct distance from the floor. It is difficult to steer the vacuum while standing on it, but the cleaner did seem to pick up dirt a little better.

When I had finished I put the cleaner back in the closet then tried to scrub the grease off my hands. With about as much success as replacing the belt.

Then I ate a handful of almonds without sharing, and took a well-earned nap.

Read 'em and Weep: My Notes to the Pet Sitter, Unabridged Version

I was waiting in line at the pet store, preparing to siphon my bank account to buy more bird treats and toys, when I spied a stack of stationery. Each packet held maybe 25 sheets, and each sheet was 4 inches by 8 inches. Each page had ruled lines and pretty pictures.

It looked to me like your typical designer stationery for people who like their letters decorated with kittens or Rottweiler's. Or maybe it was stationery for pets who enjoyed corresponding with other pets. ("Hi, it's Fluffy! Anne is helping me write this, but I was wondering if Buster could meet me at the dog park this Saturday! That is, if Buster got that procedure done last week, if you know what I mean. Wink, wink. P.S. Hope he's feeling better!") Then again, most pets probably use e-mail these days.

It turned out it was neither. Each page of the little notepad was entitled, "Notes for the Pet Sitter."

I burst out laughing so hard the bird biscuit I had been sampling almost came out my nose, causing everyone to stare. Oh, right. Like a bird owner could leave sitting instructions on a piece of paper the size of two squares of toilet paper. The phone numbers wouldn't even fit.

I mean really, let's start with the phone numbers of where I could be reached in case of emergency. There is my cell phone number, the hotel's phone number, the second hotel's number, and the cell phone numbers of any friends I might be traveling with (in case I don't answer my phone).

Then there's contact information for the vet in case one of the birds gets sick. I like to provide not only name and phone number but a color-coded MapQuest printout of the address. And let's not forget the backup vet. In case the regular vet is hit by a greyhound, I also provide the name, phone number, and MapQuested location of a second qualified avian veterinarian.

But you can't be too careful. Should the backup vet also get knocked out of commission by, say, a kick in the head from somebody's pet ostrich (hey, it could happen), I provide a backup vet, this one, unfortunately, an hour's drive away. (I live in a small town.) In my instructions I provide a break-out of how much extra I will pay the sitter for the drive time.

Then there are the backup sitters. In case my regular sitter is incapacitated -- say she walks out of the house the first morning and gets hit by a meteorite -- I arrange for a pinch sitter. (Pinch sitter, ha! Get it?) I provide both sitters with information about the other.

In the meantime, I pay the backup sitter a little something to swing by the house every evening. This serves a three-fold purpose: my birds don't get as lonely with two people looking in on them, the second sitter can feed them if the first sitter forgets, and she can hit the ground running should the first sitter collide with aforementioned meteorite.

In the terrible event something happens to

both sitters, I ask a third person to drop by the house a couple of times a week, around noon. This ensures he won't accidentally bump into either first or second sitter and absolutely ensures my birds won't starve. Unless, of course, something happens to him, too. What are the odds? Just in case, I give my cousin a key. All four people, of course, need a full set of instructions in case they become the primary sitter.

Back to those instructions. I write down where in the house to find the bird first-aid kit, complete with inventory and directions for each item. Should a bird actually need to go to the vet, I also describe where in the house to find the travel carrier.

I have this cool idea, a wise security precaution, really, along the lines of backup sitters and backup veterinarians. Some day I plan to devise a code for the travel carrier's location so a thief can't find it and use it to steal my birds. For instance, each letter in the location could also be the first letter in the name of a type of bird. Only the sitter will know what it means. Say the carrier is in the CLOSET, so I will leave in my instructions: "First letter is small gray Australian bird with crest. Second letter is long-tailed rainbow-colored bird from Indonesia with loose droppings". (Answers: cockatiel and lorikeet, C-L, and so on.) A brilliant piece of bird sitter instruction, don't you think?

Then there's the identification of each bird, also very important for optimum care. Two of the birds are easily identified by their colors, but the two grey cockatiels look so much alike no one can tell them apart except me. Differentiating between them requires a lot of descriptive such as "softer feathers" and "crooked beak you can only see by moving the feathers around the beak" and "friendly" and "not friendly."

Food is next. My birds have recently gone on food strike, deciding they hate the foods they previously loved. I have bought every brand of pellet and bird food known to the human race and I'm running out of room in my house for my own food. The birds love each new food, the first time. After that they turn up their beaks and demand something else, preferably spicy Nutriberries unless they've decided they don't like Nutriberries anymore and must now have gourmet caramel-covered popcorn.

So the instructions must detail which pellets each bird is likely to eat today and which ones tomorrow and which ones the third day. Plus the type and location of vegetables and fruits and treats. ("All perishable bird foods are located on upper right shelf of refrigerator, except for mixed frozen vegetables, a cup of which must be thawed every day and evenly distributed among the bowls. Nuts and rice on kitchen counter next to coffee maker. I made enough rice to last all week but if you run out, please cover two cups with water and cook 45 minutes. Do not drain. The birds like it to be slightly sticky.")

What goes in must come out, so next I describe each bird's normal poop. ("Sugar Franklin's tend to be a bit more watery than the other cockatiels. Charli likes to poop in one place. All poop will likely be purple should there be blueberries involved. If you see any variations, please call me at once. See telephone numbers provided above.")

Behavior and rules of the house come next and warrant an entire page. "Please do not allow any bird to chew my couch, tables, chairs, computer, books, lamps, clothes, or electrical cords," I write. Temper tantrums will ensue, but the bird sitter must be strong. Since none of my birds like any of the others, the bird sitter also must be vigilant to murderous intentions. So I include tips on locations in which to place different birds in various rooms that are most likely to maintain harmony.

Then there's entertainment. Charli likes this kind of toy, Sugar won't touch that one, Flash and Nicholas demand yet a third type. I list two or three substitute toys for each bird. Just in case. The birds must have the television on and their cages arranged in such a way as to afford the best view. The volume must not be too loud or too soft; on weekends they like to watch PBS and during the week they prefer game shows.

Petting warrants a detailed section. The sitter must pet Charli's feathers a certain way while Sugar prefers another. Flash wants nothing to do with fingers, while Nicholas blisses out at the slightest scritch. If they're molting (99 percent of the time) I must explain how each bird expresses its crankiness and ways to circumvent.

Baths? That would be nice, but I think that would be asking too much.

If I remember, I finish up with the location of the fire extinguisher and main water cutoff, trash take-out days and where to stack the mail. I ask the sitter to raise the shades in the morning so the birds can look out the window, and lower the shades again at night so they're not bothered by headlights.

All told, so far we're looking at, oh, maybe 16 single-spaced pages. Front and back. And they want me to fit this on a sheet of paper the size of an overgrown Post-it? I need more! More space and more authority to leave as many details on the care of my birds as I see fit.

Maybe paper just isn't my medium. Maybe I should leave a videotape. I could sit in a leather armchair while stroking a white Persian and laugh maniacally about birdie bread while threatening global domination if the sitter doesn't change the papers correctly. Or maybe I should leave a self-destructing audiotape with the sitter's "mission."

Then again, checking in by speakerphone every day would be warmer and fuzzier. The sitter could wear a white jumpsuit and call herself "Margie's Angel."

Or maybe I should just save a few trees and writer's cramp and bad satire and stay at home.

Ties That Failed to Bind:
Parrot Talk is Breaking Up That Old Gang of Mine

I used to have a lot of friends. Friends to eat out with, share secrets with, go to the movies with. Then I got birds, and along with the birds came new friends who had birds, too. They lived in an entirely different world, one in which life revolved around parrot behavior and nutrition, with its own subtle differences in language.

When I became a part of this world, too, most of my old friends drifted away, picking feathers out of their hair as they walked out the door.

But a few have remained, fitting into my new bird-centric life just fine. One, whom I'll call "Diane," agreed to have dinner with me and a couple of my bird friends, "Connie" and "Wanda."

As we waited for the food I told Diane how good it was to see her again and asked about everyone in the old crowd.

"Well," Diane began, "Marty got married and moved to Florida. Sally quit the factory and went back to school . . . "

"Where in Florida?" asked Connie.

"Fort Lauderdale."

"Ah," said Connie. "I know a bird breeder in Fort Lauderdale."

Wanda chimed in. "And that guy who makes the stainless steel play gyms lives in Miami."

The three of us nodded our heads in agreement.

Diane smiled politely. Then she gave me an

odd look, leaned closer and whispered, "There's something on your shoulder."

I craned my neck to see. "Bird poop," I said, shrugging. I dipped the corner of my linen napkin in a glass of water and dabbed at the spot.

Wanda continued. "Didn't they get hit by one of those hurricanes last year? Ruth or something?"

"It was Rita," Connie corrected her. "It was awful. I heard from a friend of mine that they're still finding lost birds."

The three of us shook our heads solemnly.

Diane lifted her chin delicately. "Yes, those hurricanes were awful. My brother's in the National Guard and he was sent to Mississippi." She turned to me, "You remember Dave, don't you?"

"I hear they're just going to get worse," Connie continued.

"Maybe we should prepare for one this year. Just in case," I said.

"But we don't have hurricanes in Kentucky," Diane said.

Wanda leaned toward us and said conspiratorially, "I hear global warming is going to make this area of the country very tropical."

"Think of the parrots we could keep in outdoor aviaries!" said Connie.

Diane smiled wanly.

The waiter brought our salads. Wanda beamed when she saw the fresh broccoli on her plate. "Bo Bo just loves broccoli. He'd be jumping right in my plate right about now."

"You let your birds on the table?"

Wanda looked at Diane a little sheepishly.

"Yes, I'm afraid so. But his little feet are

clean. Ever since we started using a grate in the bottom of the cage they don't get nearly as poopy."

She chuckled. "Here's what Bo Bo does when he sees broccoli." Wanda leaned over her plate, stared intently at the broccoli and slowly bobbed her head. "Mmmm! Good! Mmmm!" she said, mimicking Bo Bo. She bobbed her head more rapidly. "Mmmmm!"

Wanda's impressions of Bo Bo always crack me and Connie up, so it was several minutes before we could stop gasping and snorting with laughter.

Diane smiled and nodded at the diners looking our way. I was too busy just wiping my eyes.

Over entrées Diane mentioned that our mutual friend John had been robbed. "You know, he had that expensive security system put in, and then forgot to set the alarm."

Connie said, "Oh, no one could break into my house and live to tell about it. My two macaws can scream so loud the neighbors two miles away can hear them. Plus they bite. Hard."

"I know what you mean," Wanda said. "I've even trained my cockatoo to dial 911. You know, just in case."

Diane frowned. "You trained a bird to dial 911? Using what, its foot?"

"Beak," replied Wanda. "She says 'help' into the receiver."

Dessert was a selection of luscious fruit cobblers. I chose peach, Diane chose apple, Wanda got cherry, and Connie the blueberry. They were big servings so we all needed to-go boxes.

"My babies love blueberries," Connie said.

"Oh, you have children?" Diane asked.

"No, no kids," Connie said. I could see that her patience with Diane's inability to speak our language was wearing thin. Then she looked at her leftover cobbler and announced mischievously: "There'll be blue poop in the morning!"

"Red poop here!" said Wanda.

"Light orange for me!" I said.

Diane stood up and placed her folded napkin on the table. "I really must go," she said. "I forgot I promised to visit my mother!"

She tossed some money on the table and made a beeline for the door.

"Wow, she left in a hurry," said Wanda.

"Yeah," I said. "She never seems to have time for the old crowd anymore. It's too bad. But she never forgets her mother. Isn't that nice?"

You Talkin' To Me? Because My Birds Sure Aren't.

Birds are musical. At least, that's what I've always heard. Spring time mornings, you hear all the birds twittering and chirping and generally causing a ruckus in the neighborhood. Autumn evenings you hear them cooing to each other as they prepare to roost. Parrots are musical, too. Many of them can even sing and talk in human language. Their wonderful sounds are one of the reasons we love them so much.

Not mine, though. No, my parrots neither talk nor sing, though they do on occasion chirp softly or loudly, depending on what demands they're making of me at the time. They also screech when they're displeased, such as when I don't comply with previous demands. But singing or talking? Not a chance.

Several months ago I decided to remedy this situation. I got out all my books and scoured the Internet for how-to tips and then I began. Every day I'd whistle at Flash, sing a little song to Sugar Franklin, sing and bounce with Charli and Nicholas. Same tunes, repeated over and over and over and over, in an upbeat cheerful manner. Though, in all honesty, it's quite difficult to sing the Andy Griffith song in an upbeat and cheerful manner 3,540,719 times.

The first few times I tried this all the birds considered me with horror, backing away slowly as if I'd suddenly turned into a hideous beast with sharp dripping fangs. I'm no Roberta Flack, you understand, but I can carry a tune and my voice in no way resembles sandpaper. I considered being offended but realized they were parrots and unused to great music.

So I persevered until the birds finally stopped backing away. They then went into their bored mode. They would realize I was doing "that thing" again and then proceed to preen or stare off into the distance. Sugar Franklin even took to yawning in my face. Sometimes one of them would puff up and out, as if seized by a chill over a particular note, but none of them would utter a sound.

But I can be patient, so I continued. There I was, singing around the cages, singing with parrots on my hands or shoulders, singing along with the TV or radio, even singing to my computer. (I live alone so I don't have the inconvenience of trying to explain my behavior to "normal" people.)

Meanwhile, friends would send me pictures and sound bites of their parrots singing and talking, and the Internet discussion groups overflowed with tales of parrots yakking up a storm with no effort whatsoever on the part of their humans. Even the car dealer where my mom bought a new car had an Amazon that chatted up everyone who came in. The entire parrot world was filling the universe with wonderful sound, but the only thing to be heard in my house was me singing the Andy Griffith song and You Are My Sunshine. 3,540,719 times. Alone.

I finally gave it up, of course. Even I can take a hint. These days I content myself to imagine that my birds chat among themselves when I'm at work, that they agree among themselves as to who will be the messiest that day and who will demand the most scritches and which food they will all decide to hate for their evening meal. When I get my outrageous phone bills I immediately scan them for strange phone numbers, lest my parrots get away with calling their relatives in Australia or Africa. I know perfectly well they can talk and sing if they want to; they just won't.

Feel free to send me advice or helpful suggestions as to how you got your parrots to sing and talk with you. Just don't be surprised to get a long-distance call from one of my birds, demanding to sing or talk with your parrot while I'm safely at work. Most likely it will be the Andy Griffith song.

What Are Birds Good For? Lots of Stuff!
Put Yours to Work!

First of all, I'd like to thank all of you who responded to my last column about my birds not singing or talking. Half of you sent helpful suggestions, while the other half wanted me to know that nothing you had tried worked either. This makes me feel much better, knowing I am in the 50th percentile.

Unfortunately, none of the helpful hints have worked, possibly because I haven't tried them yet. Which, in a typically twisted way, brings me to today's topic, which is: What Are Birds Good For?

Let's be honest -- birds are nice to look at (usually), but what purpose do they serve? Of course, when I say birds I mean pet birds; wild birds provide many useful services such as eating worms and recycling old twigs into nests and waking you up from a hangover with a cheerful morning song.

Pet birds, however, expect you to keep the house worm-free and to supply them (the birds) with new and expensive nesting materials to shred all over the floor, and they only snicker at you when you're hung over.

I say it's time we make our pet birds contribute something to our lives and households. I say it's time we stopped giving and giving and giving only to receive fresh piles of poop in return. So to lead us off in the right direction, I've made a list of things that birds can easily do right now, without an expensive college education or even federal funding.

Use your bird's beak to unscrew things. For example, last year I bought a new office chair and worked for hours putting it together, tightening all the nuts and bolts, and hammering in screw caps flush with the surface so that nothing could get to the bolts and unloosen them. Within five minutes, Charli, my brown-headed parrot, had easily removed all the screw caps and unscrewed all the bolts. Then calmly waited for me to sit down in the chair with no bolts.

If you're tired of breaking your nails on the layers of plastic encasing today's modern products, turn your bird loose on the dang stuff. Once again, those sharp beaks can come to the rescue, with the added benefit of shiny plastic shards flung places the vacuum won't go.

Pet birds are amazingly adept at moving objects from one place to another. Whether it's a plastic bottle cap, a spear of asparagus, or your last two quarters for the newspaper, there's nothing like watching it being tugged, thrown, pushed, or dragged to a new, more appropriate position. Such as down the heating vent. Why not harness this dexterity for cleaning up the kitchen after a meal, straightening up your desk, or teaching your bird to move checkers for you?

Cockatiels are excellent carpet cleaners. Those little beaks can pull seed husks and potato chips from between the fibers better than any vacuum on the market.

Birds are your ticket to an exciting career in the art world. Molted feathers can be fashioned into fanciful headdresses or exotic dancer costumes.

Glue Zupreem, feather dust, strips of newspaper and claw clippings to canvas to create whimsical "found object" pieces. ("I call this Residue of Cockatoo.") Start your own Jackson Pollack revival by allowing your bird to stroll through dinner guests' plates, then set him on a blank canvas. Watch out, New York MOMA!

Own a thriving home-based business? Can your bird say "hello"? (Sure she can! That's *all* she can say, the lazy little beggar!) Save money on temp help during busy periods by using your talking bird to answer the phone. What customer wouldn't be charmed to be greeted by, "Step up" or "Poop"?

Suspect your mate or best friend is trying to poison you? Birds are natural food tasters. Heaven forbid Petey should take a bad burrito for you, but let's face it, he is more than willing to lay down his life for a chance at your grub. Might as well take advantage of it.

For those of you who sport a beard or moustache, nothing beats a bird for cleaning your facial hair of wayward bits of food. Afterward your bird can comb out each strand barbershop neat! Think anesthesia is for sissies? Many parrots also offer mole and freckle removal.

Birds are a great boost to the local economy via the vet's office and pet stores, but how about improving your personal economy? Consider train-ing your bird to leave evenly spaced beak marks on the leaves of your houseplants, which you can then sell as rare flora at ridiculously high prices.

You have a house full of dark, ancient furniture (sometimes known as "antiques")? A bird can turn it into something useful: decorative toothpicks. Nothing sells on eBay like bulk shipments of shredded mahogany or walnut.

Those pesky telemarketers who ignore the national Do Not Call list can be put right with just one blast of a well-timed parrot screech.

If economic times are *really* bad, put your bird to work stealing jewelry from houseguests. Sure, you might lose a friend or two, but can you help it if your bird likes carats? I mean really. Anyone with half a brain knows that, to a bird, diamond stud earrings are like a neon invitation: RIP ME OUT WITH YOUR BEAK! PLEASE! No one should go prancing around wearing gaudy bling bling like that to begin with. Teach your bird to palm the loot under a wing until he can meet you for the drop.

You think your bird is weird, the way he stares for hours at "nothing there?" In reality, your house is infested with invisible beings and he is trying to protect you. Be grateful! This is one bird who is earning his keep.

Yes, birds can enrich our lives in a variety of ways. All we have to do is take advantage of their many, many talents.

You Want Smart? Forget Dogs.
Let's Talk About Parrots!

Some German researchers discovered a couple of weeks ago that dogs recognize human language. Evidently this is huge news to this handful of scientists, who apparently have never seen a dog, much less had one take up residence in their home. What will the scientific community come up with next? Cats are independent?

So a dog recognizes what we say to him. Big deal. A dog knows the word for bone or treat. It's not like we use enormous vocabularies when we talk to dogs -- we rarely say more than "bone," "treat," or "good dog!" We don't sit around and discuss the current state of world affairs with our dogs, or at least when we do we don't expect any answers.

Of course, this is absolutely no surprise to you parrot owners -- I can see your smug faces right now. You're thinking, "Hey, my parrot not only recognizes human language, but has also given me the secret to balancing the federal budget. Let's see some dog top that!"

I agree, because I, too, have parrots. As I've mentioned before, they don't actually talk to me, but their behavior has assured me that they are the most intelligent creatures on the face of the earth. I say that with only slight reservation, because sometimes my parrots do odd things. For example, Charli, my African brown-head, likes to back herself into the corner of her cage, stick her feet behind her head and flip herself over. It's a pretty neat trick, but she frequently forgets how to get herself untangled.

From dropping in on Internet chat rooms and Usenet I have learned that many of your parrots are also the most intelligent creatures on the face of the earth, even when they are doing odd things. One owner wrote a heartwarming post of how her conure begs for paper plates. When she complies and gives the conure a paper plate, the conure wrestles it into submission, sticks her head under the plate, then rises up like a goddess from the sea wearing a paper plate hat. Perhaps the conure believes herself to be more attractive to potential mates thusly attired. Or perhaps she is just weird.

For extreme examples of intelligence we must go to the cockatoos and macaws. Let's begin with Glacie, whose human slave is named Toni. "Glacie has learned a new trick. She has learned to take the nuts off the screws and take the doors off her cage . . . all the doors. She even understands the process -- lefty loosey, righty tighty. She doesn't even bother trying to turn them to the right now. She knows that's not how they work."

Then there's Sydney, the Mollucan cockatoo who got so good at opening her cage latches that her human, Cary, put one of those little three-roller combination locks on her cage, the kind you put on a suitcase. Within a couple of days, Sydney had learned the combination and "within three minutes she would be out on top of the cage cackling and bouncing up and down, quite pleased with herself."

Alex wrote in to explain how his blue and gold macaw liked to open his small food and water doors, until he got bored with how little noise and mess that made. He then decided it was a lot more fun to take the entire door with bowls off and drop the whole works on the floor. Of course, Alex tried using a wrench to tighten the bolts, but you macaw owners already know the result of that.

The next illustration of animal intelligence comes from rec.pets.birds. Another blue and gold regularly dismantles her food and water dish holders, ensuring that her human gets plenty of exercise cleaning things up. One day the human left the house with the macaw securely locked in her cage and the cat napping on the window sill. When the human returned the cat was securely locked in the bird cage and the macaw was contentedly preening on the window sill. Let's see a dog top that!

By far the most chilling example of avian intelligence has been revealed to us by Ellen's love bird, Pepper. This bird has taken to carrying a plastic dish over her back and head, even eating and drinking with the dish balanced on her body. Ellen has thoughtfully provided pictures of this at http://loveofbirds.com/p&r/Pepper1.htm.

What is so disturbing about this so-called new behavior is that Pepper is teaching it to other love birds. Between you and me, it looks like these love birds are practicing wearing protective gear, such as plastic dishes, that they will need during the coming parrot takeover of earth.

If I were you I would start sticking plastic dishes over my head, too. And maybe one over your dog's head. Just in case.

Christmas at Mother's, with Bird

I hope everyone had a great holiday; I can hear those sighs of relief from here.

This year I got brave for my annual Christmas trip to my mom's. She lives about 80 miles away, far out in the country in a town with a population of less than 2,000 people.

I decided to take Charli, my brown-head, with me. She loves to travel.

Once she realized we weren't going to the vet's she liked it even more. She hung upside down in her cage and watched my driving with a critical eye and a bemused expression on her face. About halfway to mom's I took Charli out of her cage and let her sit on my shoulder. Which Charli loved, but which also made her car sick.

Parrots fly, for heaven's sake, yet they get carsick?

Of course, I had to put her right back in her cage, where she hung upside down again, though you'd think that position would not be beneficial for car sickness.

I should probably explain here that my mother tolerates my parrots. She is of a mind that all animals belong outside, animals do not possess any of the human traits I keep insisting they have, and that I have spoiled my birds beyond endurance. No one ever treated a chicken like a pet when she was growing up, she enjoys reminding me.

The first time I took a bird to my mom's house, it was my lutino cockatiel. My mother is a wonderful country cook, and as usual, she'd outdone herself. The table was loaded with hot and steaming bowls of vegetables and breads and so on. Before dinner I took my cockatiel out of her cage to explain that I'd be giving her some good food in a few minutes -- when she flew out of my hand, across the room to the table, and landed perfectly in the mashed potatoes.

My mother did the silent back stiffening she only does when horrified. I grabbed the cockatiel, gently wiped off her little feet, and put her back in her cage. Then I scooped up the "dirty" portion of the potatoes where the bird had landed, so as to not contaminate the remaining potatoes. Mother watched this, then picked up the bowl and scraped all of the potatoes in the trash. She got a clean bowl from the cabinet and filled it with the remaining potatoes that had been left on the stove.

So I was determined there would be no more incidents regarding parrots and food in my mother's presence. I put Charli in her travel cage on a table in the middle of the living room, in full view of the kitchen and all the food. We were even able to have a few bites before the pitiful chirps began. I got up and carefully prepared a tiny dish of mashed potatoes, green beans, peas, and a bit of homemade yeast rolls, which I carefully placed in her cage. My mother watched in silence, shaking her head.

Charli viewed this offering first with one eye and then the other and decided it was a poor substitute for what the humans were having. Normally, I'd just have Charli out to share my meal in her own dish, but I knew better than to suggest that to my mom. So Charli just had to chirp pitifully until we'd finished dinner.

Then it was time to open presents and watch TV and gossip. It was also safe to get Charli out of her cage, though I did insist she at least get one molecule of a vegetable near her beak. As if psychic, she smeared her beak through the mashed potatoes in her food dish.

I put Charli on my knee (where she promptly cleaned her beak on my jeans) and scritched her feathers for awhile. Then I gently bounced my leg so Charli had a little parrot ride on my knee.

Mother pursed her lips but kept quiet.

When I got home I called mom to let her know the trip back was uneventful and to firm up the plans for after-Christmas shopping. I mentioned that when we got home Charli immediately climbed into her Hide 'n Sleep and went right to sleep.

My mother's sigh came through the phone perfectly. "Well yes," she said, "I can see where she'd be tired after all that bouncing on your knee."

"She did have a big day," I protested. "That long trip to a new place, a strange house, and so on."

My mother just said "Uh huh."

How Shakespeare Really Did It

It's sad, really. We give our parrots shelter, food, and toys. We talk to them and play with them. We make fools of ourselves singing off-key and making faces to amuse them. I myself have been overtaken this past month by molted feathers, an excessive egg-laying cockatiel with an impacted and inflamed preen gland, and two male cockatiels who have taken the art of night frights to new heights. I can live with the lack of sleep and the piles of feathers drifting across the floor, and even the expense of hormone shots.

But for many of us, things have gone too far.

I know a man who received a beautiful, luxurious expensive robe for his birthday. Only the bird doesn't like it, so the man cannot ever wear the robe again.

A woman lately announced on a listserv that her parrots insist on standing on her (the woman's) feet when she showers, and then on her knee when she attempts to shave her legs. She uses a lot of band-aids.

Then there is the man who had to give up his dog because the wife's parrot kept terrorizing it.

And the graduate student who can't study in her apartment because the parrot keeps eating her books and papers, and the professors aren't buying that old "But my bird ate it" excuse.

These incidents are not accidents, nor are they isolated. I've been keeping track of them, and I'm starting to have night frights myself.

But that's not what this column is about. No, what this column is about is giving credit where credit is due.

Parrots are responsible for a lot of things: the bird toy industry, the wasted vegetable co-ops, the rising stock prices of millet companies. But I'll bet you didn't know that parrots are responsible for the enduring works of Shakespeare, did you?

Consider -- an African grey scratches at the bottom of its cage as ole' Bill sits nearby trying to think of a suitable piece of dialogue. The grey scratches and scratches as if trying to erase something. Aha! "Out out, damn spot!"

A love bird takes a fancy to Bill and begins inserting useful bits of chewed-up paper and twigs in Bill's beard. The Scribe has to spend a lot of time untangling himself from the bird and ridding his beard of foreign objects. Later, as Bill writes in his "Thought for the Day" diary with the ocean scape on the cover, he says, "Oh, what a tangled web we weave . . . "

One of the more contrary Amazons of that era was forced to bathe by William's wife (bet you didn't know he (Shakespeare) had a wife either, huh?), whereupon the Amazon announced, "What fresh hell is this?"

You want the real truth on where the idea for Romeo and Juliet came from? It was based solely on a love triangle between three macaws. Granted, none of the macaws stabbed themselves or drank poison, but the Bard watched the entire matings and betrayals between the parrots work themselves out.

It turned out all right, of course, for the macaws. The abandoned macaw soon found true love in a neighbor's macaw. In fact, the offspring from that pair are still living in upstate New York, running a quaint bed and breakfast with an Old English motif.

Then there was the Gang-Gang cockatoo perched outside Mr. and Mrs. Bard's cottage, happily munching on brilliant red fruits. The bird's joy was obvious. While Mrs. Shakespeare refreshed her supply of facial creams from the lady on Avon, Bill scribbled down, "My love is like a red, red rose." I am aware that berries do not resemble red roses, but I don't think spectacles had been invented yet.

Revenge was not a topic Billy had given much thought to. Until his Senegal began stalking the pigs in the back yard. The pigs attacked, of course, so the Senegal flew inside and pouted while he planned his revenge. Thus, Hamlet was born.

Watching these events and feeling vastly superior to both human and parrot, the raven cawed "Oh what a piece of work is man!" And then flew off to visit his old pal, Edgar, who had a bust over his study door that hadn't yet been pooped on.

Just Another X-Rated Day At My House

It was a morning like any other. I was late (again) and as I was rushing out the door I thought I saw a sudden movement in Flash's cage.

I stopped and stepped backward. Yep, Flash was busily enjoying himself on one of the heated perches I'd gotten him for his feet.

I know it's natural, and I know parrots could care less what you think of them, but it stayed on my mind all day.

If Flash was using an object that's supposed to help his feet feel better to make other parts of himself feel better -- what next?

Was Flash going to start a porn ring in my house? Would I come in early one day to find cockatiels with names like "Soft Cinnamon" or "Feather Crazed" lounging around the cages, indolently stretching their wings? Cockatiels already have orange cheeks -- would I get a mysterious bill for facial feather rouge? How long before they realized that water only lasted so long as a way to shine up a beak? What lengths would they go to to find beak enhancing sheen stick? Or feather dye?

It wouldn't stop there, of course. Soon there would be the videos and podcasts. Tiny cameras scooting around the carpet, capturing the best angles. Exotic parrots of all sizes and colors, arriving day and night in front of my house, stepping out of garish colored Barbie Doll limos.

Strange moaning squawks heard around the neighborhood. Would children peer in the windows and see groups of parrots piled on top of one another?

Just how small can chains and whips get?

How would they handle the paparazzi? Would they hire love birds to guard the premises and act as bodyguards? Would they let me in my own house?

There would have to be a 900 number, of course, for those unfortunate souls who couldn't make the trip in person. It would be staffed by throaty greys, closing their eyes as they intone, "hmmmmm thass good" or "gimme all that millet, baby."

And what about the times a parrot wouldn't be able to perform? Has avian medicine invented the little blue pill for parrots? How does it work? Would one dose suit all, male and female alike?

With any big money-making industry there's always the risk of organized crime moving in. Would Flash be blackmailed by the Gang of Gang Gangs or forced to deal in illegal drugs? How would I know which one was the narc?

Would I end up in jail as contributing to the delinquency of a parrot or illegally importing Quakers?

Flash is finished with his heated perch, for the moment at least. But there's a gleam in his eye I'm not sure I like. Excuse me while I go pop several aspirin.

Make It Easy On the Birdies

This is a great country. A land of creativity and innovation and vision. A land where free spirits have given us items that give us a life of ease and an attention span of 20 seconds. A land where you can make zillions from the stupidest idea imaginable, and possibly win prizes for it, too.

But it's time now, I think, to turn our attention to the parrots. For too long now, parrots have suffered from a lack of implements and appliances that would make their life easier and free them up to fully express their own creativity.

Here are some of the ideas I've had after eating half a bar of dark chocolate with 77% cocoa content:

A Molt Meter
A gently chirping meter that lets all humans and other birds know when it's molting season. This would prevent those too frequent scritches that brush against tender blood feathers, resulting in the bird having to bite its human and then the tedium of having to listen to the human whine.

Automatic Nest Finder
This handy device will take the work out of exploring every dark nook and cranny in the house by measuring the light, depth, width, and height of all areas of a room. When a suitable area is found (based on the bird's special requirements) a signal will go off. This signal will not be audible to

humans, freeing the bird to furnish its nest without the knowledge or interference of its humans.

Automatic Scritcher

If there's one universal among parrots, it's the incessant need to be petted and scritched and preened. Since most humans must work a few hours a day for money to buy treats, an automatic scritcher can fill those gaps when the humans are absent or are in the hospital having their fingers rebuilt.

Healthy Food Sorter

This remarkable invention will take the labor out of finding vegetables and fruits and other undesirable foodstuffs that the human may mix into seed mixtures. The abhorrent foods will automatically be thrown to the floor.

Vet Terminator

A sophisticated marvel that senses the proximity of veterinary offices and, once within range, destroys all swabs, needles, syringes, probes, and other instruments of avian torture. Humans are not harmed by the Terminator since they (the humans) do occasionally supply scritches and treats.

Toy Rater

We've all had the experience of buying expensive toys that all parrots like, except our parrot, who becomes deathly afraid of it. The intensity of the fear and loathing is directly proportional to the cost of the toy. The Toy Rater will take the work out of examining the toy for scary parts and transmit the information to the bird. The bird will then choose the degree of fear to exhibit to the human. This clever device will also work with toys that do not frighten the bird at all, allowing the parrot to amuse itself by tormenting the humans in the environment.

In the great spirit of American ingenuity I am offering you the following challenge: Send us your idea of the most useful appliance or gadget or implement that would make your parrot's life easier. We do not care about making your life easier, remember, because you are only the human. Just your bird's life.

The reward, you ask? I will be glad to send you a handful of molted cockatiel feathers. And, because this is America, there's always the astronomical chance an entrepreneur with far too much money will read this column and feel the need to force millions of dollars upon you (please contact me privately to determine the amount of my commission).

Come on, America! Show us your best!

www.ingramcontent.com/pod-product-compliance
Lightning Source LLC
Chambersburg PA
CBHW060416050426
42449CB00009B/1984